D1261511

WITHDRAWN

# ON THE HUNT WITH
# GRIZZLY BEARS

BY NANCY FURSTINGER

**The Child's World®**
childsworld.com

Published by The Child's World®
1980 Lookout Drive • Mankato, MN 56003-1705
800-599-READ • www.childsworld.com

Acknowledgments
The Child's World®: Mary Berendes, Publishing Director
Red Line Editorial: Design, editorial direction, and production
Photographs ©: Shutterstock Images, cover, 1, 13; Gleb Tarro/Shutterstock
Images, 4; Andre Anita/Shutterstock Images, 7; Greg and Jan Ritchie/
Shutterstock Images, 8; Eric Wang/Shutterstock Images, 10; iStockphoto,
12, 17; Antoni Murcia/Shutterstock Images, 14; Red Line Editorial, 16; Dieter
Meyrl/iStockphoto, 18; Erik Mandre/iStockphoto, 20; Dennis W. Donohue/
Shutterstock Images, 21

ISBN 9781634074520

LCCN 2015946217

Printed in the United States of America
Mankato, MN
December, 2015
PA02279

# TABLE OF
# CONTENTS

# Chapter 1

# HUNTING FOR SALMON

A grizzly bear trots down a mountain in Alaska. Her two cubs trail behind. It is the first day of summer, but the air is chilly. The bear family winds its way through pine trees. At the bottom of the mountain, a big river sparkles in the sun.

The big **sow**, or female, is hungry. She dug up nuts this morning. But they did not fill her. Her cubs growl. They want a meal. The sow knows they need much more food. They will need to live off of their body fat during the winter.

The mother bear needs to fish. Each year grizzlies gather to feast on salmon. The salmon arrive in late June. The fish come in from the ocean. Then they swim upstream. Many salmon return to the river where they were born to lay their eggs.

Knowing this, the mother bear and many other bears flock to the river. Huge **boars**, or males, fight for the best fishing spots.

◄ Grizzly bears seek out spots along rivers where the most salmon swim.

The mother bear roars at a boar that comes too near. The male bear could be a danger to her cubs. Boars are fierce **predators**. They may even kill bear cubs.

The mother bear finds a spot for her and her cubs to fish. Then she steps into the river. Her hungry cubs wait on the shore. She watches the salmon. They swim fast and close to the surface. The fish are high in fat. This fat will help the grizzlies gain weight. Females like this mother can weigh up to 660 pounds (300 kg). Males can weigh up to 1,500 pounds (680 kg).

The mother bear dives under the water. She is a skilled swimmer. She swims underwater for some time. Soon she spots something shiny in the water. It's a salmon! Snap! She snatches it in her jaws. This is just one way grizzlies catch fish. Some use their paws to trap fish at the bottom of the river.

The cubs pace along the shore, waiting for their meal. The mother bear shows them how to hunt for food. She also teaches them how to avoid danger. Then she will send her cubs off on their own.

The mother drops her catch on the shore. The cubs feast. Then she returns to the river to catch more salmon. She needs to feed herself, too. Adult bears can eat up to 30 fish per day. Early in the season they eat every bit of the fish. The hungry bears

Grizzly bears are skilled at swimming and fishing. ▶

even eat the tail. Later, when the bears are less hungry, they only eat the fatty parts. They eat the brain, skin, and eggs inside the fish. Adult bears like this mother eat up to 90 pounds (41 kg) of food each day. This will help her gain around 6 pounds (3 kg) per day.

The two cubs gobble the fish. Then they wrestle on the shore. The female cub wins the match. She bats at the fish in the river. The male scratches his back against a tree. The mother returns with her own catch. Her cubs snatch bites. Today's fishing proved successful. Tomorrow the three bears will return to the same spot on the river.

◄ **A mother grizzly shares her catch with her cubs.**

# Chapter 2

# BULKING UP

After the surge of salmon, the mother bear and her twin cubs seek out new sources of food. They focus on gaining weight for the coming winter. Right now it is summer. There is plenty of food for the bears to eat. The female cub finds a blackberry patch. She gobbles up the sweet fruit. Soon her fur is stained purple. The male cub watches as a field mouse pops out of the ground. He pounces on the mouse. It makes a tasty snack. Meanwhile, their mother crunches ripe apples.

The sow and her cubs are at the top of the food chain. They can eat almost anything. Grizzly bears are **omnivores**. Their diet can change from day to day. Most of their meals are made up of plants. They eat seeds, leaves, roots, fruits, and nuts. But bears also eat meat, such as fish and other mammals. Some of their **prey** is tiny, such as mice. Other prey is very large. Bears hunt bison, elk, and moose. They target young or old animals. These are easier to catch.

◄ **As omnivores, grizzly bears eat both meat and plants.**

▲ Long, sharp claws help grizzlies dig for plants and insects.

The bear family climbs up a mountain. Many bears gather at the top. They have come to munch moths. The insects bury themselves in dark gaps. The bears dig up the moths. It takes many moths to fill each grizzly's stomach. The mother and other adults can eat up to 40,000 moths in just one day.

The mother and her cubs lick the last moths off of their arms. Then they curl up. It is nap time. The sun glimmers on their fur. Their long brown fur has silver tips. This gives the fur a grizzled or gray look.

As autumn approaches, the grizzlies keep eating as much as they can. The mother follows a swarm of bees back to their hive.

She uses her five sharp claws to rip the honeycomb from the hive. Then she and her cubs feast on the honey. They also gobble up bees. The angry bees try to sting the bears. But the bears' fur is too thick. The cubs yelp when the bees sting their ears. They shake bees from their fur. Then it is time to leave. The bear family will need all of their energy to dig a **den**.

▲ Grizzly bears earn their name from their grizzled, gray fur.

# Chapter 3

# A LONG WINTER SLEEP

It is October. It is time to get ready for winter. The bears roam across their home range in North America. Female bears and their cubs live in ranges up to 300 square miles (777 sq km). Males have much larger ranges. These might be as big as 500 square miles (1,295 sq km).

The bears leave messages to mark their range. Their home overlaps with the homes of other grizzlies. The mother bear's older cubs live nearby. Cubs go off on their own when they are two or three years old. Many stay close to home. First the mother and her young cubs rub against trees. They leave behind their scent. This wards off other bears. They also scratch and scrape the bark. These marks signal that the bears live here.

The mother's first job is to find a spot for her den. Some mother bears use hollow trees. Others use caves. This sow digs

◄ **A mother grizzly bear rubs her scent on a tree to mark her territory.**

Grizzly bears live here

▲ Grizzly bears live in many northern countries.

out a den in a hillside with her claws. She also uses the hump on her shoulders to help her dig. The huge hump has strong muscles. This makes the sow's shoulders powerful. Her cubs help. They drag in branches and leaves. These make cozy beds.

Soon the first flakes of snow fall. The bears start to settle into their dens. Pregnant females enter dens first. Females with cubs follow next. Then it is time for single females to go into their dens. Males are the last to settle in.

The bear family curls up for a full winter of deep sleep. Their heart rates slow down to ten beats per minute. Their sleep might last up to six months. Sometimes bears wake up to find food. But like all grizzlies, the mother and her cubs can live off of their fat. They won't need to leave the den during the winter.

Halfway through the winter, another female in her den gives birth. Most often, grizzlies have two to four cubs. This mother is having twins. Each tiny cub weighs only 1 pound (.5 kg). The cubs snuggle for warmth. They have very fine hair. They don't have teeth yet. Their eyes are sealed shut. The cubs will **nurse** on their mother's milk for the rest of winter. The new mother and her cubs will be the last grizzlies to leave their den in the spring.

▲ **This mother grizzly has found a cave to use as her den.**

# Chapter 4

# STARTING A NEW CYCLE

Finally it is spring. The new cubs have opened their eyes. They have also grown fur and teeth. It is time to leave the den. The bear family slowly wakes up. They stretch and yawn. They leave their den with one thought: find food. The bears have lost much of their body weight over the winter. They need to eat.

The new mother bear sniffs out a meal. With her keen sense of smell she can smell dead animals and other food miles away. The mother tracks the scent. Her cubs follow. All three are hungry.

Soon they find the body of an elk. The elk died during the harsh winter. A wolf pack has already eaten part of the elk. Now the mother bear and her cubs eat. Once they are full, the mother digs a huge hole. She drags the elk into the hole. She buries it down deep. The bears will return to their leftovers when they need to eat again.

◄ **The first order of business after waking is finding food.**

As the mother bear curls up for a nap, her cubs play. They wrestle and tumble down a hill. This play is fun. It is also important for their survival. It teaches them to pay attention and to act when needed. This will help them stay safe in the forest.

The mother bear isn't asleep that long when her eyes snap open. She senses danger. Her sharp ears hear branches crashing. She rears up on her hind legs. She stands tall at 8 feet (2.4 m). This helps her to get a better view. She spots a male grizzly.

▲ **Playing and wrestling with each other helps cubs learn how to be alert and protect themselves.**

▲ **Grizzly bears roar to fend off other grizzlies.**

The mother bear grunts to warn her cubs. She chases her cubs up a tree.

Like other bears, this mother will do anything to protect her cubs. Her main job is keeping her cubs safe. If she needs to, she will fight off other animals. Even male bears. The mother bear growls and roars. She is very angry. Her nose is raised. Her ears are flattened. She frightens the male bear away.

Soon the bears will **breed**. The male bears will wrestle. They will bite one another with their sharp teeth. They fight to see who is the boss. The top boars will breed with female bears. When the male cub is around five years old he will join in these fights. Someday he could become a top boar.

# GLOSSARY

**boars (BORS):** Boars are adult male bears. Boars fight each other for the best fishing spots.

**breed (BREED):** To breed is to produce offspring. Male and female grizzlies breed between May and July.

**den (DEN):** A den is the home of a wild animal. The mother grizzly bear dug her den into a hillside.

**nurse (NURS):** To nurse means to feed offspring with milk from a breast. The mother grizzly bear will nurse her cubs all winter.

**omnivores (AHM-nuh-vors):** Omnivores eat both plants and animals. Grizzly bears are omnivores.

**predators (PRED-uh-terz):** Predators are animals that eat other animals. Grizzly bears are predators at the top of the food chain.

**prey (PRAY):** Prey are animals that are eaten by other animals. Grizzlies sometimes steal prey that a wolf pack has killed.

**sow (SAU):** A sow is an adult female bear. The sow becomes dangerous when an animal disturbs her cubs.

# TO LEARN MORE

## Books

Miller, Debbie S. *Grizzly Bears of Alaska: Explore the Wild World of Bears*. Seattle: Sasquatch Books, 2014.

Sartore, Joel. *Face to Face with Grizzlies*. Washington, DC: National Geographic, 2007.

Trueit, Trudi Strain. *Grizzly Bears*. Mankato, MN: Amicus, 2015.

## Web Sites

Visit our Web site for links about grizzly bears: childsworld.com/links

*Note to Parents, Teachers, and Librarians: We routinely verify our Web links to make sure they are safe and active sites. So encourage your readers to check them out!*

# SELECTED BIBLIOGRAPHY

"Bear Viewing at Brooks Camp." *National Park Service*. National Park Service, n.d. Web. 13 May 2015.

"Grizzly Bear." *National Geographic*. National Geographic, n.d. Web. 16 May 2015.

"Grizzly Bear." *National Wildlife Federation*. National Wildlife Federation, n.d. Web. 25 May 2015.

# INDEX

# ABOUT THE AUTHOR

Nancy Furstinger is the author of more than 100 books. She has been a feature writer for a daily newspaper, a managing editor of trade and consumer magazines, and an editor at children's book publishing houses. She lives in Upstate New York with a menagerie of animals.